The Defense of Wisconsin 2006 Marriage Amendment (Theses)

By

Terry Virgil

The Defense of Wisconsin 2006 Marriage Amendment (Theses)

by

Terry Virgil

07/09 /2014

Abstract

The assault made on the Wis. Const. amend. art. XIII, § 13, by the same-sex idea of marriage must end, and traditional marriage between just one man and one woman only is to be upheld in the United States of America; liberal federal judges have no right to make any law[s] according to U.S.Const. art. III, for U.S Const. art. I § 8.cl.1-20 even says that the federal government is very limited. Therefore the federal government is also limited in the jurisdiction of what it can do. The assault by same-sex marriage cases in federal court is a direct violation of U.S. Const.amend.X, and U.S.Const. amend I. Avery clear cases of the assault on Wis. Const. amend. art. XIII, § 13 by same-sex marriage. It demands that the federal government is the only type of government that can determine whether same-sex marriage is to be legal, and not should not be up to the federal judges. This should be up to the States like it has been, for if U.S. Const. amend. X is okay for the States that has made same-sex legal then it is legal for States like Wisconsin to do the same, for the United State Constitution is the same for all States not a select few. The State of Wisconsin has the right to say no to same-sex marriage.

Unit 9 Assignment, Final Project (Theses)

Protection of Traditional Marriage as Between One Man and One Woman

In 2006, the State of Wisconsin banned same-sex marriages and all same-sex civil unions in an Amendment to the State's Constitution. This constitutional provision must be upheld against political assault, because it protects the true fabric of the America family unit and is a lawful exercise of State's Rights preserved in U. S. Const. Art.I § 8.cl.1-20, U.S. Const. amend.X. of the U.S. Constitution.

Introduction:

According to those who wrote and developed the United States Constitution and the Bill of Rights, the primary concern was to protect of States Rights as well as individual[s] rights. The main and only idea was to have the States to determine just what individual[s] Right[s] is to be in each individual State. This would include the right to determine who and who is to be recognized as a legal marriage, for the State of Wisconsin did just this in 2006 with the Wis. Const. amend. art. XIII, § 13, for the State of Wisconsin has every right to do so under the U.S. Const. amend. X; this means that the State of Wisconsin did comply with the law[s] and did not violate any and all law[s] that are in the United States of America Constitution according to the principle of the founding fathers and that was ratified in 1789 by all the States.

If one would review the U. S. Const.art.I § 8.cl.1-20, also known as the Twenty Enumerated Powers of the Federal Government, a person would see that very limited powers have been granted to the federal government. The federal government is limited so as to give the States the right to determine how the federal government is to deal and do things not the federal government dictating to the States on how and what to do when it comes to the States making a law[s]. A law by the State of Wisconsin banning same-sex marriage is no exception to the U.S. Const. art. I § 8.cl.1-20 and U.S. Const. amend. X.

The U. S. Const. amend.X, reinforces just what U. S. Const. art. I§ 8.cl.1-20, does say; "hands off" to the federal government when a State likes Wisconsin wants to make their own law[s] pertaining to marriage just between one man and one woman only.

The United States of America Supreme Court does not have a constitutional right to make a ruling against the State of Wisconsin when in truth the United States Supreme Court would be in a direct violation of both U. S. Const. amend.X, U. S. Const. art. I§ 8.cl.1-20 in addition to U.S.Const. art. III; therefore seeing that a federal judge did indeed to make a law that same-sex marriage is to be legal in the State of Wisconsin, and the State of Wisconsin has no right to make any law[s] even a State Constitution change that would ban same-sex marriage. That is why the federal judge's ruling must be over turned, and Wisconsin's 2006 State Constitution must be reinstated, and the federal government must reimburse the State of Wisconsin for any revenue that has been lost. The biggest revenue that would be lost is entitlements that all liberal like same-sex couples and civil unions would cause. In order to support same-sex marriage with civil unions' taxes would have to be increased by about 500% to around 850% with more tax law[s] to be added in order to increase the State of Wisconsin's budget each year. All same-sex marriage that have been made are to be held as illegal and all those that come from a State whereby same-sex marriage is legal should not be recognized as a legal marriage. The Federal judge that made this ruling should be held both accountable and responsible for a deliberate, willful violation of U.S.Const. art. III, X, U. S. Const. art. I§ 8.cl.1-20, U. S. Const. amend.X, by the State of Wisconsin filing a law suit against that one federal judge, or even filling charges against that federal judge for violating the "States Rights" under U. S. Const. amend.X, and any other charges that can be made and filled.

The other fact that same-sex marriage does assault is the family and the way the State of Wisconsin does define just what a family is by law, for both the federal judge and same-sex marriage does remove the smallest form of government which is a family. To rule against traditional marriage between just one man and one woman only does mean the end of what a family is, for a family is made up to be parents of the opposite sex (gender) and a child or children that are blood related or adopted. Wis.Stat. 108.04(7) (s) 1(b) is the law that does define just what a family is in the State of Wisconsin. This is one other reason why Wis. Const. amend. art. XIII, § 13 must be reinstated by overturning the federal judge's ruling so that the assault on the Wis. Const. amend. art. XIII, § 13 has end and same-sex marriage is defeated once and for all.

The one threat that same-sex marriage makes on society is in the area of forcing people to accept their way of life if a person happens to disagree with the life style of a same-sex couple that is pretending to be legally married when in truth they are not a married couple. With the very same idea same-sex marriage would mean that ever Christian Church on earth would have to change their legal doctrine in order to allow a same-sex marriage in their church, for the Founder of the whole Christian Church does not allow same-sex marriage in His Church. Along with the Founder of the Whole Christian on earth would have to change the policies and the way each church school teaches and their doctrine, to include home schools, private, charter schools, and any other school that is not a public school in order to comply with same-sex marriage law[s]. This would mean U.S. Const. amend. I would have to be changed to say the federal government can establish a nation or federal church; therefore the President of the United States would have to declare them self as better than the Founder of the Whole Christian Church on earth.

These are just a few reasons why Wis. Const. amend. art. XIII, § 13 is and should be found to be Constitutional, and no federal judge has the right under the Constitution according to U.S. Const. art. III and U.S. Const. amend. X even if a federal judge is a liberal or bias judge, for no federal judge is above the law.

The Importance to The Rule of Law:

Reviewing the purpose of why there is a need to uphold the 2006, Wisconsin Constitutional Amendment against all political assault would be to not just protect the true fabric of a family (the fabric of a traditional marriage between just one man and one woman only), but show that fact the a centralized federal government in truth is not why the founding fathers fought for our freedom in the Revolutionary War; instead to keep the United States of America a small federal so that the States have the "States Rights" to make their own laws, and to make law[s] for the individual[s] in their own States, for this is the purpose of U.S.Const.art.1§ 8, U.S. Const. amend. X of the Constitution of the United States of America. U. S. Const. amend. I does state all individual[s] have the right to choose freedom to be free, and not in the slavery of a communist style type of government or in a monarchy, or to have same-sex marriage ideas forced onto them. Same-sex marriage does violate the principle of U. S. Const. amend. I with the backing of the President of the United States of America. 81 Fordham L. Rev. 619, Copyright (c) (2012) Fordham Law Review; Joseph Landau, I. The President and DOMA, "On February 23, 2011, the Obama Administration announced that it would no longer defend the constitutionality of DOMA section 3" According to U.S.Const. art II § 4 the President of the United States of America is to enforce the law[s] and not break or no longer defend the law[s] in which was signed into a law by another President of the united States of America. The fact is the President of the United States of America is not above the law, for they are to be held equal to the law, for no human being is above the law. The law is for every human being to obey this includes the leaders that are appointed to represent a nation such as the United States of America. The President of the United States has no right under the U.S. Const. amend. X to even violate "States Rights", for each State in the United States of America has a constitutional right to make and enforce their own law[s] which they feel is necessary to govern the people of that State in which they live in. Wisconsin is one of those States in which the President of the United States of America has no right to say he will ignore the Constitution that guaranteed under U.S. Const. amend. X, and by saying he will not enforce 1 U.S.C. A. § 7; therefore the State of Wisconsin has every right to sue the President of the United States of America for the violation of U.S.Const.amend.X, or to ask Congress for articles of impeachment against the President of the United States as a free and sovereign States can do according to the United State Constitution. This would include charging the President of the United States with criminal charges and to be tried by the United States Senate. U.S. Const. art. II § 4 "The President, Vice President and all civil officers of the United States, shall be removed from office on impeachment for, and conviction of, treason, bribery, or other high crimes and misdemeanors."

1 U.S.C. A. § 7 is a law that has to be enforced by the President of the United States of

America, for this is the duty of the executive branch of office in either the State government or the federal government of the United States of America. This is one of the checks and balances of government. Just because the President of the United States does not like a law that does not give him/her the right to violate any and all law[s].

The real reason why this is so relative to the legal field and legal profession is because in order to defend the sovereign right to have a State Constitutional Amendment or law[s] to determine who has the right to marry such as a traditional marriage between just one man and one woman only, thus the State of Wisconsin has very sovereign right to have a Wis. Const. amend. art. XIII, § 13 as a law for the citizens of the State of Wisconsin only. In addition the legal field and legal profession can defend the sovereignty of the people of the State of Wisconsin to make their own law[s] as they feel fit to do so, and not to be dictated to by a President of the United States America and the federal courts by saying there is no more "States Rights" under the U.S. Const. amend. X. This is a very liberal idea for the President of the United States and federal courts to say and have the U.S. Const. amend. X so that they can have their way to promote same-sex and have traditional marriage between just one man and one woman only like Wis. Const. amend. art. XIII, § 13 does state.

<u>The traditional marriage between just one man and one woman only, and how it is to be defined:</u>
The 2006, Wisconsin Constitutional Amendment (Marriage Amendment). To review the words that make it very clear that the Wisconsin Constitutional 2006, marriage amendment is legal, for time to review.

 [created as of Nov. 2006] Wis. Const. amend. art. XIII, § 13 "Only a marriage between one man and one woman shall be valid or recognized as a marriage in this state. A legal status identical or substantially similar to that of marriage for unmarried individuals shall not be valid or recognized in this state".

The reason for this 2006 marriage amendment and it real purpose is to protect and defend just what is a family and how a family is to be defined so the government of the State of Wisconsin can defend a family like it is, also according to the idea and truth of just what a government is, and how a government is to function as a true republic.

Lincoln, A. (1863, November 19). Gettysburg address, in *Collective Works of Abraham Lincoln: Speeches and Writings,* Balser, R., Ed. Retrieved from http://www.abrahamlincolnonline.org/lincoln/speeches/gettysburg.htm

. These words were spoken by President Lincoln in 1863, the Gettysburg Address, "that this nation, under God, shall have a new birth of freedom -- and that government of the people, by the people, for the people, shall not parish from the earth."

These great words that was spoken by President Lincoln did mean just one thing that this is a republic nation and not a nation whereby a dictator, monarch or just one person, or group rules, but a nation whereby a represented voted into office that would represent fifty-one percent of those that are edible, and not a liberal action of just a few like those in favorite of same-sex marriage. This would also mean that the federal courts President of the United States of America cannot interfere with the rights of each State[s], and the laws that they create in order to govern themselves by. The same would go as U.S. Const. Preamble "We The People" even would mean that this nation is a republic, not a dictatorship, not ruled by a monarch. Same-sex marriage would end the republic type of rule that the United States of America has endured for the past two hundred thirty-eight years. The end of the republic means States have no more "States

Rights", no more freedom to choose, for every citizen of the United States of America would have to agree with same-sex even if they disagree, for it is very clear that same-sex marriage is the beginning of either a dictatorship, or a monarch type of government for the United States of America.

Wis. Const. amend. art. XIII, § 13 is a law that can prove each State does have "States Rights", for this State Constitutional Amendment was written in obedience with U.S.Const. amend.X, meaning that the State of Wisconsin did comply with the Constitution of the United States of America, and that the words from President Lincoln form his Gettysburg address does hold true that in order to be a republic that the people of the State of Wisconsin have every right to make their own laws as they feel fit to do. It was the people of the State of Wisconsin that voted this into law November 2006, by a margin of eighty percent of the people in agree meant to have Wis. Const. amend. art. XIII, § 13 as part of the Wisconsin Constitution.

Wis. Const. amend. art. XIII, § 13 did defeat the veto by then Governor Jim Doyle after he vetoed the Wis. Const. amend. art. XIII, § 13 twice, and it was the people that defeated then Governor Jim Doyle by having Wis. Const. amend. art. XIII, § 13 on the ballot to be voted on by the people; therefore it was the people's choice and not a dictatorship of monarchy rule by a Governor.

The reason for this 2006 marriage amendment and it real purpose is to protect and defend just what is a family and how a family is to be defined so the government by their own government, for a government is the organization that is to protect a family all members of a family even the unborn, for the reason is a family is the smallest form of a government. This is why when there is "States Rights" like it says in U.S.Const. amend.X. then with "States Rights" does come individual rights, for it is the State that have every right to give individual right and not the federal government.

Wis. Const. amend. art. XIII, § 13 is a "States Rights": therefore no federal judge and not even the President of the United States of America even has the right to determine if the State of Wisconsin is to be forced to allow same-sex marriage or not. In truth not even the United Nations has a right to force the State of Wisconsin to allow same-sex marriage.

It is very clear that those whom appose Wis. Const. amend. art. XIII, § 13 in the name of equality just have no respect for just what a traditional marriage is and the meaning of just what a traditional marriage represents. A traditional marriage with just one man and one woman only does represent just what a traditional family is under Wis.Stat. 108.04(7) (s) 1(b) "'Family Member' means a spouse, parent[s], child or a person related by blood or adoption to another person.'"

Same-sex marriage cannot be even identified as a traditional family under the State of Wisconsin or be classified as a family under Wis.Stat. 108.04(7) (s) 1(b). Again this does violate Wisconsin's the right to make their own law[s] under U.S.Const. amend. X. Same-sex marriage would also have Wis.Stat. 108.04(7) (s) 1(b) declared as unconstitutional as well.

This fact is truth as well that same-sex marriage cannot even identify just who a husband or who a wife is like it is defined under a federal law 1 U.S.C.A. § 7 signed into law by President Clinton in 1996.1 U.S.C.A. § 7 " 'marriage' means only a legal union between one man and one woman as husband and wife, and the word 'spouse' refers only to a person of the opposite sex who is a husband or a wife.'' The opposite sex is a reference to the beginning of a family which is the beginning of small government, and the small government is to be protected under

U.S.Const. amend. X. A person that is of the same-sex is in violation of 1 U.S.C.A. § 7 because there is no spouse according to the definition of what is a "spouse" that was given in 1 U.S.C.A. § 7. It for these truths that same-sex marriage should not even be recognized as a legal marriage couple, for there is no definition of opposite sex indicting just who is the "spouse" is. This is one area that same-sex marriage has never even and cannot even identify with.

Wis. Const. amend. art. XIII, § 13 can prove that only one man and one woman only does mean that there will be another generation of human beings to come into the world so there will be another generation to follow, and there is no proof that a same-sex couple can even produce another generation in the most natural way.

1 U.S.C. A. § 7 the proof made by the federal government that was signed into law 1996 By President Clinton that would state another generation of human beings can only come from a traditional marriage just between one man and one woman only, and just there is no proof that a same-sex married couple can even produce another generation the natural way. This Federal Act does back up both Wis. Const. amend. art. XIII, § 13, Wis.Stat. 108.04(7) (s) 1(b). No same-sex married couple has ever even been able to produce a natural hire. A legacy is a naturally born hire from a traditional marriage just between one man and one woman only.

<u>The Defense of Marriage Act (DOMA) signed into law 1996.</u>

DOMA states, "determining the meaning of any Act of Congress, or of any ruling, regulation, or interpretation of the various administrative bureaus and agencies of the United States, the word 'marriage' means only a legal union between one man and one woman as husband and wife, and the word 'spouse' refers only to a person of the opposite sex who is a husband or a wife'' 1 U.S. C.A § 7

The words that are in this Federal Act would back up the 2006 Wisconsin Constitutional Amendment, because of the fact that the Wis. Const. amend. art. XIII, § 13 was model after 1 U.S. C.A § 7 in the way to say that a marriage was to be just one man and one woman with the idea that a husband is a man and a wife is a woman.

The fact that both Defense of Marriage Act (DOMA) and Wisconsin's 2006 Marriage Amendment does not state anything about "civil unions" or same-sex marriage does have the key words in both to say a traditional marriage is the will of the people the keys words are "spouse" meaning the opposite sex found in DOMA which is more defined in Wisconsin's 2006 Marriage Amendment with these key words "just one man and one woman" meaning a spouse of the opposite like it is stated in 1 U.S. C.A § 7.

Definition of a same-sex couple:

To define or give definition just what is the meaning of same-sex couple is very clear to define is a person that is attracted to a person of the same-sex or gender such as a woman to another woman or a man to another man. An unnatural learned behavior that has been around for the last five thousand years since all human beings have been on the face of the earth.

Hamer D. (2012 February 14) An open letter on Homosexuality to My Fellow Scientist in Uganda kristof blog.nytimes.com Retrieved from http://kristof.blogs.nytimes.com/2014/02/20/an-open-letter-on-homosexuality-to-my-fellow-ugandan-scientists/?_php=true&_type=blogs&_r=0

"President Yoweri Museveni of Uganda is about to sign into law a vehement anti-gay law after "medical experts presented a report that homosexuality is not genetic but a social behaviour," according to a tweet from Ofwono Opondo, a Ugandan government spokesman."

February 5th, 2011, Politifact, Rhode Island, "Massachusetts public schools teaches kids as young as kindergartners about gay marriage." Young children in the State of Massachusetts, and Rhode Island public schools are taught about same-sex marriage; therefore again this is a taught trait and or idea and it is not a natural thing that comes from birth for a child must learn how to have a sexual relationship with the same-sex person.

Definition of just what a family is:

Wis.Stat. 108.04(7)(s)1(b) "Family Member' means a spouse, parent[s], child or a person related by blood or adoption to another person.'"

Wisconsin does define just what a family consist of with the following key words are "spouse", parent[s], related by blood, adapted to another person. Spouse would go back to 1 U.S. C.A § 7, for the word spouse is a word that does and is the opposite sex person in order to have the begging of a family whereby children can be produced from.

According to both 1 U.S. C.A § 7, Wis.Stat. 108.04(7)(s)1(b) there cannot be a definition of a family with a same-sex marriage, because there is no way for any and all same-sex marriages to have the existence of the key words that are to be found in both 1 U.S. C.A § 7, Wis.Stat. 108.04(7)(s)1(b); these key words are all legal words that does define just what a family is.

To have "States Rights" for a State to be able to make a definition or to determine just is a family is a constitutional right that is found under U.S.Const. amend. X; therefore the State of Wisconsin does have every right to make a law[s] in the area of protection of a family by identifying what a marriage is to be under Wis. Const. amend. art. XIII, § 13 and a family is under Wis.Stat. 108.04(7)(s)1(b). This does show that a same-sex marriage cannot be a legal family under Wis.Stat. 108.04(7)(s)1(b); therefore any same-sex marriage that enters or crosses the borders of the States of Wisconsin even a civil union cannot be recognized by the States of Wisconsin. If a same-sex couple with an adopted child come from another State where same-sex marriage is legal. According to Wisconsin law[s] the same-sex couple would have to forfeit and surrender that child or children to the legal authorities of the State of Wisconsin if they decide to be a residence of the State of Wisconsin, because the State of Wisconsin does not recognize any and all same-sex marriage[s] for other States where same-sex marriage is legal in the State where the same-sex married couple came from. All of this means that a same-sex marriage and civil union is to be made null and void, therefore each person is a same-sex marriage is now a legal single person, and each child is too adopted out to a traditional marriage couple whereby a marriage is just between one man and one woman only.

This is a "States Right" that the State of Wisconsin would have under U.S.Const. amend. X to enforce if the State of Wisconsin chooses to do so.

No liberal federal judge or even the President of the United States of America has the right to dictate to the State of Wisconsin how to define just what a family is or is not to be.

States' Rights:

U.S.Const. amend. X " the powers not delegated to the United States by the Constitution, nor prohibited by it to the States, are reserved to the States, respectively, or to the people"

According to these words as they are written it is very clear that the States' have more constitutional rights than the federal government. Even under U. S. Const. Art.I § cl.1-20 has the very same meaning as U.S.Const. amend. X.

If a liberal federal judge makes a ruling that would states that a State has a law[s] is to be considered unsensational that judge cannot make any law[s] such as making same-sex marriage legal in a State like Wisconsin whereby the people of the State of Wisconsin voted the 2006 Wisconsin to be a State of Amendment by saying same-sex marriage is the law. This ruling should not be valid, because the liberal federal judge did willfully and delivery violates U.S.Const. art. III. The liberal federal judge should have ruled that (2006) Wis. Const. amend. art. XIII, § 13 be taken back to the people of the State of Wisconsin so the people so the citizens of the State of Wisconsin can make their would law[s] to determine a legal marriage in their own State.

The President of the United States of America cannot even violate U.S.Const.amend.X, or even take it upon himself to even make a statement with words or subject that same-sex marriage is to be legal in all fifty States, for such words are a direct violation of U.S.Const. art II § 4. Such words are an impeachable act where by the President of the United States of America and can be charged for impeachment, for "The President, Vice President and all civil officers of the United States, shall be removed from office on impeachment for, and conviction of, treason, bribery, or other high crimes and misdemeanors." U.S.Const. art II § 4. President of the United States of America is to enforce the law that is their power according to the Constitution of the United States of America; therefore the President of the United States of America cannot make any words to the effect that they will not honor or enforce a law such as 1 U.S. C.A § 7; by saying word to the effect same-sex marriage should be legal, the President states that. It is okay to violate the law at will. The President of the United States would be saying there is no longer any more "States Rights" under U.S.Const.amend.X. this would mean that the President of the United States of America is just like the Dictator of North Korea. By also saying that same-sex marriage should be legal in all fifty States would also be a violation U.S.Const. amend. I "Congress shall make no law respecting an <u>establishment of religion, or prohibiting the free exercise thereof; or abridging the freedom of speech</u>, or of the press; or the right of the people peaceably to assemble, and to petition the government for a redress of grievances." An establishment of religion by the President of United States of America would be if same-sex was to be made legal, for there would be no more freedom of religion in the United States of America, for it would be illegal for an religion group, church, or an organization that does appose same-sex marriage to even exist. Every traditional marriage between just one and one woman would no longer be a legal marriage in the united States of America even if the Founder of the whole Christian church on earth say it is so. Freedom of speech depends on the freedom of religion, for without freedom of religion there is no freedom of speech or even the right to peacefully assemble without any government interference. No U.S.Const. amend. X without the freedom of speech or religion.

<u>Twenty Enumerated Powers of The Federal Government: U.S. Const. art. I § 8. cl.1-20:</u>

U. S. Const. art.I§ 8.cl.1-20 is a law written for the federal government to obey because This very law meaning is the fact that the federal government is to be held only to be very limited, and according to what is written in this law means that the States have more jurisdiction and even more power over the federal government. Those every State has "States Rights" and the freedom to tell the federal government what to do and what the federal government cannot and cannot do.

It is very clear with U.S. Const. amend. X and U. S. Const. art.I§ 8.cl.1-20 that every State in the union has the constitutional right to determine their own marriage law[s], and who has the right to be legally married in their own State. It is also clear that the powers of the federal government can be remover or even restricted if the boundary of the one[s] does violate both U.S. Const. amend. X and U. S. Const. art.I§ 8.cl.1-20 or any part of the United States Constitution, for not no human being is above the law.

Discuss sources:

Utah's State Marriage Law:

Utah. Const. art.I .§ 29(1)(2), " (1) Marriage consists only of the legal union a man and a woman. 2) No other domestic union, however denominated, may be recognized as a marriage or given the same or substantially equivalent legal effect."

Seven words in the State Constitution of Utah does define just what is a legal marriage in the State of Utah. Making it illegal to have any other type of marriage such as same-sex marriage in the State of Utah, and the State of Utah will not recognize a union of same-sex marriage or any other type of marriage in the State of Utah.

The State of Utah is a State whereby the federal courts and the President of the United States of America does demand to force same-sex marriage in order to violate Utah. Const. art.I .§ 29(1)(2); therefore the State of Utah's "States Rights" guaranteed under U.S.Const. amend. X, U. S. Const. art.I§ 8.cl.1-20 along with U.S.Const. amend. I. The violations by both the President of the United States and liberal federal judges along with liberal federal courts must be stopped.

Texas State Marriage Law:

Tex. Const. art.I § 32(a) "Marriage in this state shall consist only of the union of one man and one woman."

Again another State that has its Constitutional Rights violated by a liberal federal judge And the President of the United States of America whereby the State of Texas has no right to make their own laws concerning legal marriage in their State. The violation of U.S.Const. amend. X, U. S. Const. art.I§ 8.cl.1-20 along with U.S.Const. amend. I must end.

Wisconsin, Utah, Texas, Pennsylvania are a few States that have stood up to against the President of the United States of America, the liberal federal judges and liberal federal courts by just using "States Rights" and the meaning of "States Rights" according to U.S.Const. amend. X.

Seventeen out of the fifty States say people of the same-sex can legally be married, yet it is legal for these States to have their "States Rights" according to U.S. Const. amend. X, but it is not legal for the other thirty-three States to determine their own marriage law[s] or State Constitutional Amendments according to U.S. Const. amend.X, for there is no "States Rights" for the thirty-three States that disagree with same-sex marriage. The meaning of this means a minority has more rights under the United States Constitution v. the majority. The other part of this meaning is that a minority is the only one[s] that can make the law[s] even law[s] how one is to live, think, say, act, or even do anything.

Oregon v. The United State Supreme Court Case No. 6:13-cv-01834-MC

Or. Const. art. 15, § 5(a) "**Policy regarding marriage.** It is the policy of Oregon, and its political subdivisions, that only a marriage between one man and one woman shall be valid legally recognized as a marriage. [Created through initiative petition filed March 2, 2004, and adopted by the people Nov. 2, 2004]"

Mapes J. (2014, April 17) Openly gay judge, Michael McShane, in spotlight overseeing Oregon Case. Oregon Live: The Oregonian. Retrieved from http://www.oregonlive.com/mapes/index.ssf/2014/04/gay_marriage_openly_gay_judge.html

"Starting next week, the spotlight on the status of gay marriage in America will shift to the Eugene courtroom of U.S. District Judge Michael McShane – who finds himself in an unusual position.

Unlike the five federal judges who have struck down laws prohibiting same-sex marriages in other states in recent months, McShane won't have anyone in the courtroom defending Oregon's constitutional ban when he holds oral arguments Wednesday.

And, unlike the other judges, McShane also happens to be one of just nine openly gay members of the federal judiciary, according to the Human Rights Campaign"

The liberal federal judge should have his ruling challenged based on the fact this liberal federal judge is gay. and seeing that same-sex marriage is for the gay community only. That would mean that the liberal federal judge would base his ruling on a biased fact. This would be another violation by a liberal federal judge that can be found under U.S. Const.art.III, plus a very willful act of violating U. S. Const. Art.I § cl.1-20 8; therefore case *Oregon v. The United State Supreme Court* Case No. 6:13-cv-01834-MC should have been dismissed or a conservative federal judge should have been allowed to hear the case. A liberal federal judge is not above the law even one that is on the same side as same-sex marriage legal teams are on.

Pennsylvania v. The united States Supreme Court:

Pa. Const. tit. 23 part II § 1102. Definitions "The following words and phrases when used in this part shall have the meanings given to them in this section unless the context clearly indicates otherwise: **"Department."** The Department of health of the Commonwealth. **"Marriage."** A civil contract by which one man and one woman take each other for husband and wife. **"Marriage license"** or **"license."** A license to marry issued under this part.(Oct. 16, 1996, P.L.706, No.124, eff. 60 days)"

Pa. Const. tit. 23 part II § 1704 "**Marriage between persons of the same sex.**It is hereby declare d to be the strong and longstanding public policy of this Commonwealth that marriage shall be between one man and one woman. A marriage between persons of the same sex which was entered into in another state or foreign jurisdiction, even if valid where entered into, shall be void in this Commonwealth (Oct. 16, 1996, P.L.706, No.124, eff. 60 days)"

Geidner C.

(2014, May 20) Federal Judge Strikes Down Pennsylvania Same-sex Marriage Ban: buzzfeed.com Retrieved from

http://www.buzzfeed.com/chrisgeidner/federal-judge-strikes-down-pennsylvania-same-sex-marriage-ba

"WASHINGTON — For the second day in a row, a federal judge — this time in Pennsylvania —has struck down a state ban on same-sex couples' marriages. Less than 24 hours after U.S. District Court Michael McShane — an Obama appointee — struck down Oregon's state constitutional amendment barring same-sex couples from marrying, U.S. District Court Judge John E. Jones III — appointed to the bench by President George W. Bush in 2002 — reached the same ultimate conclusion in Pennsylvania. "We now join the twelve federal district courts across the country which, when confronted with these inequities in their own states, have concluded that all couples deserve equal dignity in the realm of civil marriage," Jones wrote. Like McShane in Oregon, Jones provided for no stay of his ruling, meaning it goes into effect immediately — and same-sex couples should be able to apply for marriage licenses immediately, although there is a three-day waiting period to get the license. Although Pennsylvania has no constitutional amendment barring same-sex couples from marrying, Jones on Tuesday struck down the state's 1996 statute banning same-sex couples from marrying and barring recognition of out-of-state marriages of same-sex couples. As to his legal conclusion, Jones wrote, "[W]e hold that Pennsylvania's Marriage Laws violate both the Due Process and Equal Protection Clauses of the Fourteenth Amendment to the United States Constitution. Because these laws are unconstitutional, we shall enter an order permanently enjoining their enforcement. By virtue of this ruling, same-sex couples who seek to marry in Pennsylvania may do so, and already married same-sex couples will be recognized as such in the Commonwealth."

It seems to be the case or part of the argument that it is every liberal federal judge so far is and only the very far left winged just like the so very far left winged liberal President of the United States of America in this case the very far left winged President Obama have gone with the determination to not just to hail insults to the traditional marriage between just one man and one woman only, but to remove not just the dignity of a human being, but also to throw insults against the Constitution of the United States of America and all fifty States in the Union.

It is also very clear that every liberal federal judge has a fear of going against the President of the United States of America just like a judge would do in the nation North Korea. The plain fact and truth is all liberal federal judges that have been violating U.S. Const.

art. III, U. S. Const. Art.I § cl.1-20, U.S.Const. amend. I, U.S.Const.amend.X, 1 U.S.C. A. § 7, and removed from the beach under U.S.Const. art II § 4.

United States v. Windsor No. 10 CIV. 8435 (BSJ) (June 6, 2012)

Background: "Woman brought action seeking a refund of federal estate taxes levied on her same-sex spouse's estate and a declaration that section of the Defense of Marriage Act (DOMA) defining "marriage" as a legal union between one man and one woman as husband and wife violated equal protection. After the Executive Branch decided not to enforce DOMA, a congressional group was allowed to intervene to defend the constitutionality of the statute, 797 F.Supp.2d 320. Subsequently, woman moved for summary judgment and congressional group moved to dismiss." regulation, or interpretation of the various administrative bureaus and agencies of the United States, the word "marriage" means only a legal union between one man and one woman as husband and wife, and the word "spouse" refers only to a person of the opposite sex who is a husband or a wife."

The right word is spouse, for in order to be a spouse one must have or be identified as a husband or a wife the word husband must mean a male (man), and a wife is a female (woman) in order to be united as a married couple. Not in this case two women "claiming" to be a married couple, for the two women in this case is not even a heterosexual couple, for they are only two individuals that is single according to the law.

This case does prove that the same-sex people have no right to even claim an inheritance, for the fact is same-sex marriage has never even have a definition for just who is a spouse not one has ever been identified as a wife or a husband or the opposite sex like in 1 U.S.C.A. § 7. It is truth that with same-sex does remove the very reason for having a traditional marriage in the first place, for in order to have any inheritance there first has to be one person to be identified as a wife of a husband; therefore seeing that a same-sex couple can be identified as an individual only there is no marriage between a same-sex couple because of the fact there is no one who can be identified as a "spouse". No "spouse" means no marriage.

California Bath Room and Locker Room Law (AB 1266):

To remove traditional marriage just between one man and one woman only then there are immoral law[s] that are made legal because the minority groups or organizations demand equal rights like same-sex marriage is demanding. The other fact and truth is law[s] like the California bath room, locker room law like any same-sex law[s] does open the door to more crime, and more problems in society. The one word and identification that is removed is heterosexual, or how to separate the difference between a male or female. Just like the word "spouse" in 1 U.S.C.A. § 7 does identify who a wife or husband is that same would go for man and woman in Wis. Const. amend. art. XIII, § 13, Or. Const. art. 15, § 5(a), Tex. Const. art.I § 32(a), Utah. Const. art.I .§ 29(1)(2).

Cal. Const. amend.chap.85.§ § 221.5 (a)(b)(c)(d)(e)(f) "(a) It is the policy of the state that elementary and secondary school classes and courses, including nonacademic and elective classes and courses, be conducted, without regard to the sex of the pupil enrolled in these classes and courses.(b) A school district may not prohibit a pupil from enrolling in any class or course on the basis of the sex of the pupil, except a class subject to Chapter 5.6 (commencing with Section 51930) of Part 28 of Division 4 of Title 2. (c) A school district may not require a pupil of one sex to enroll in a particular class or course, unless the same class or course is also required of a pupil of the opposite sex. (d) A school counselor, teacher, instructor, administrator, or aide may not, on the basis of the sex of a pupil, offer vocational or school program guidance to a pupil of one sex that is different from that offered to a pupil of the opposite sex or, in counseling a pupil, differentiate career, vocational, or higher education opportunities on the basis of the sex of the pupil counseled. Any school personnel acting in a career counseling or course selection capacity to a pupil shall affirmatively explore with the pupil the possibility of careers, or courses leading to careers, that are nontraditional for that pupil's sex. The parents or legal guardian of the pupil shall be notified in a general manner at least once in the manner prescribed by Section 48980, in advance of career counseling and course selection commencing with course selection for grade 7 so that they may participate in the counseling sessions and decisions.(e) Participation in a particular physical education activity or sport, if required of pupils of one sex, shall be available to pupils of each sex.(f) A pupil shall be permitted to participate in sex-segregated school programs and activities, including athletic teams and competitions, and use facilities consistent with his or her gender identity, irrespective of the gender listed on the pupil's records."

<u>Reviewing the second paragraph of the (Declaration of Independence):</u>

U.S. Declaration of Independence, Paragraph 2 (1776) ""We hold these truths to be self-evident, that all men are created equal, that they are endowed by their Creator with certain unalienable Rights, that among these are Life, Liberty and the pursuit of Happiness.--That to secure these rights, Governments are instituted among Men, deriving their just powers from the consent of the governed, --That whenever any Form of Government becomes destructive of these ends, it is the Right of the People to alter or to abolish it, and to institute new Government, laying its foundation on such principles and organizing its powers in such form, as to them shall seem most likely to effect their Safety and Happiness."

The same-sex marriage idea happen to use the "pursuit of happiness" clause to demand, mandate, and control their right to marriage a person of the same-sex. Yet the people of the same-sex marriage idea just forgot about one thing, and that thing is the United States of America is a republic and not a communist nation like they would like to see.

To change the principle of traditional marriage just between one man and one woman only does mean every legal citizen of the United States of America would also have to change their right to "pursuit of happiness" to be the very same as a same-sex marriage would, for in order to even have a "pursuit of happiness" every legal citizen of the United States of America would have to be first identified as not a heterosexual human being, but as a homosexual human being. To be a heterosexual would have to be a crime according to the policy or idea of same-sex marriage, and those liberal federal judges that go along with violating U.S.Const. art. III, U.S.Const. art II § 4, U.S.Const. amend. I, 1 U.S.C. A. § 7, Wis. Const. amend. art. XIII, § 13, Tex. Const. art.I § 32(a), Pa. Const. tit. 23 part II § 1102, Pa. Const. tit. 23 part II § 1704,Or. Const. art. 15, § 5(a), Utah. Const. art.I .§ 29(1)(2), and U.S. Const. amend. X the most. Without U.S. Const. amend. X there is no such thing as the "pursuit of happiness" no freedom to be free this is what same-sex marriage does, and likes to do. Same-sex marriage is not freedom to be free.

<u>First Amendment to the Constitution of the United States of America:</u>

U.S. Const. amend. I "Congress shall make no law respecting an establishment of religion, or prohibiting the free exercise thereof; or abridging the freedom of speech, or of the press; or the right of the people peaceably to assemble, and to petition the government for a redress of grievances."

To have same-sex marriage legal in the United States of America, the U.S. Const. amend.

I would have to be abolish completely in order to commentate the religion that same-sex marriage brings about, because same-sex couples all love the idea of not having any and all heterosexuals the right to freedom of speech. It would have to be illegal to be a heterosexual in the United States of America if same-sex marriage is the be legal according to the liberal federal judges and President Obama. It is this reason and reason alone why the U.S.Const. amend. I has got to be removed to allow same-sex marriages legal in every State of the union, because same-sex marriage would demand, force, and mandate all hate crimes, plus all hate crimes is a violation of the U.S.Const. amend. I with just one word, and that word is freedom.

The other freedom that has to be removed because of the belief same-sex marriage is the freedom that comes from the Founder of the Whole Christian church that is on earth. Freedom comes from the Found of the whole Christian church on earth, and not one human being that would be found on the earth.

The political assault on traditional marriage between just one man and one woman only:

The political assault made by the people that are in agreement of same-sex marriage or the liberal federal judges or President Obama are the ones that would like to see U.S.Const. amend. I removed alone with the U.S. Declaration of Independence, Paragraph 2 (1776), for they love to see either a monarchy or a dictatorship type of government, and have "States Rights" like it say in U.S.Const. amend. X.

Landau J. (2012) The Obama Administration Decision To Defend Constitutional Equality Rather Than The Defense of Marriage Act 81 Fordham L. Rev. 619, Fordham Law Review; retrieved from Westlaw (approx. 19 pages) http://campus.westlaw.com.lib.kaplan.edu/result/previewcontroller.aspx?TF=756&TC=4&mt=CampusLaw&db=1142&ordoc=2028227528&caseserial=2028227528&rp=%2ffind%2fdefault.wl&findtype=1&spa=004042837-2000&serialnum=0377627421&vr=2.0&fn=_top&sv=Split&pbc=BC6E23F9&casecite=133+S.Ct.+2884&rs=WLW14.04&RP=/find/default.wl&bLinkViewer=true

"President Obama's decision not to defend DOMA is based on a narrow and fundamental ground."

The main part of the political assault is the freedom of religion in which is the foundation of the United States of America, and the main principle and cause to why the United States of America became a free nation with freedom in the very first place.

Johnson C. (1994-2013) MayflowerHistory.com. Retrieved from

http://mayflowerhistory.com/mayflower-compact/

"In ye name of God Amen· We whose names are vnderwriten, the loyall subjects of our dread soueraigne Lord King James by ye grace of God, of great Britaine, franc, & Ireland king, defender of ye faith, &c Haueing vndertaken, for ye glorie of God, and aduancemente of ye christian ^faith and honour of our king & countrie, a voyage to plant ye first colonie in ye Northerne parts of Virginia· doe by these presents solemnly & mutualy in ye presence of God, and one of another, couenant, & combine our selues togeather into a ciuill body politick; for ye our better ordering, & preseruation & fur=therance of ye ends aforesaid; and by vertue hearof, to enacte, constitute, and frame shuch just & equall lawes, ordinances, Acts, constitutions, & offices, from time to time, as shall be thought most meete & conuenient for ye generall good of ye colonie: vnto which we promise all due submission and obedience.

In witnes wherof we haue herevnder subscribed our names at Cap=Codd ye ·11· of Nouember, in ye year of ye raigne of our soueraigne Lord king James of England, france, & Ireland ye eighteenth and of Scotland ye fiftie fourth. Ano: Dom ·1620·"

Same-sex marriage, liberal federal judges, and even liberal Presidents do not like the freedom of religion because of the fact there is a freedom of choice. The freedom to choose like the Pilgrims did in 1620 against the right to freely worship God as they felt fit to do, and not like a King or Dictator would like them to do. It is this very freedom that believers in same-sex marriage, liberal judges, even the President of the United States of America hate the most, for by having a political assault against such freedoms like religion means no more republic, for the liberal President can step in and declare themselves as the dictator or new monarch, and the path would be cleared by same-sex marriage with the help of the liberal judges that have ruled against traditional marriage between one man and one woman only. The fact is same-sex marriage is a political assault on the true fabric of all freedom and not just the freedom of religion. Freedom of religion is the key to the freedom of speech, and the key to a free republic.

Conclusion:

Wis. Const. amend. art. XIII, § 13, is a legal amendment that was made and has been established by the people of the State of Wisconsin according to the idea of "States Rights" according to U.S.Const. amend. X, U. S. Const. Art.I § cl.1-20 with the very same principles that is found in 1 U.S.C. A. § 7, Pa. Const. tit. 23 part II § 1102, Pa. Const. tit. 23 part II § 1704, Or. Const. art. 15, § 5(a), Tex. Const. art.I § 32(a), Utah. Const. art. I. § 29(1)(2), would be true that the State of Wisconsin has every right to make their own law[s] as the State of Wisconsin feels fit to do, for the very principle of the first Ten Amendments to the United States

Constitution meaning is the States have to right to guarantee who gets the individual rights and not the federal government under the first ten amendments. By looking at different States law[s] this is the proof that each State in the United States has the right to determine their States law[s] concerning who can and cannot get marriage in those States. Wisconsin is one of those States whereby the liberal federal courts along with the President of the united States of America who want to deny the State of Wisconsin the right to make their own law[s] or State Constitutional Amendment to the State Constitution as the State feel fit to do.

It is very clear to say that the liberal federal judges will not uphold any state law that says a marriage is to be tween just one man and one woman only, because the fact every liberal federal judge so far has struck down each and every law[s] or State Constitutional Amendment like Wisconsin's Wis. Const. amend. art. XIII, § 13, therefore in truth every liberal federal judge is in direct violation of U.S.Const. art. III in addition to U. S. Const. Art.I § cl.1-20 by saying there is no such thing as "States Rights" as it is found in U.S. Const. amend. X. It is clear in U.S.Const. art. III that the only type of ruling a liberal federal judge should give out is an interpretation of any law or State Constitutional Amendment, and not making law[s] like they have been doing in their liberal rulings against the United States Constitution itself.

In truth liberal federal judges along with the President of the United States of America displayed a willingness audacity to willfully disobey and fine ways to violate the Constitution of the United States of America in such a way that would bring about just one thing, and that thing is a second civil war that has already been declared by the heinous idea of same-sex marriage. Liberal federal judges are paving the way to end "States Rights" as we would find it in

U.S.Const .amend. X by declaring law[s] like Wis. Const. amend. art. XIII, § 13 unconstitutional; therefore the liberal federal judges are in truth and saying to the people of Wisconsin that they have no constitutional rights to have any "States Rights" and U.S.Const. amend. X does no longer even exist and is no longer valid any more, plus the President of the United States of America can now come in and dictate to the State of Wisconsin that a new federal guideline is in place whereby same-sex marriage is the law and there is no more religious rights, for the liberal federal judges and the President of the United States of America have stated that all religions have to preform same-sex marriages. This is the establishment of religion President Obama has indicated with his words that they must be and forced onto the people of United States same-sex marriage is to be legal. It was the freedom of religion that the pilgrims wanted in 1620 as it is shown in the "Mayflower compact of 1620" this very fact.

Freedom to choose is an "unalienable right' and not a right given to another human being, for another human being cannot grant freedom to any and all human beings on the face of the earth. To say U.S.Const. amend. X is unconstitutional by the liberal federal judge and the President of the united States of America is not freedom for the States to have a right to make a law[s] or State Constitutional Amendment allowing States not to allow any same-sex marriage like the State of Wisconsin did in 2006 with the (2006) Wis. Const. amend. art. XIII, § 13.

The fact is both the President of the United States of America and the liberal federal Judges are pointing the United States of America to a communist type of government control by telling States like the State of Wisconsin cannot have their Constitutional Amendment Wis. Const. amend. art. XIII, § 13 prohibiting same-sex marriage.

Wis.Stat. 108.04(7) (s) 1(b) does defines just what a legal family is in the State of

Wisconsin the help of a legal way to identify a family is in the words of 1 U.S.C. A. § 7, and the word "spouse" along with the meaning of the word "spouse" by defining the word "spouse" as one of the opposite sex (gender) is the start and only way a family can come about, for in a same-sex marriage there is no "spouse" or a definition of just what is a "spouse" with the idea and definition of opposite sex (gender). This would mean that every human being in the United States of America including the State of Wisconsin is the same-sex (gender) making everyone equal. This should mean that every human being is either a woman or a man and not both. Seeing that the liberal federal judges along with President Obama have said that law[s] like Wis. Const. amend. art. XIII, § 13, and 1 U.S.C. A. § 7 are all unconstitutional means no more family. Without any family there is no marriage, and no more government to run, no longer will there be any human beings left on the face of the earth. This is what same-sex marriage will do is end life on earth.

Bibliography

Mapes J. (2014, April 17) Openly gay judge, Michael McShane, in spotlight overseeing Oregon Case. Oregon Live: The Oregonian. Retrieved from

http://www.oregonlive.com/mapes/index.ssf/2014/04/gay_marriage_openly_gay_judge.html

Geidner C. (2014, May 20) Federal Judge Strikes Down Pennsylvania Same-sex Marriage Ban: buzzfeed.com Retrieved from

http://www.buzzfeed.com/chrisgeidner/federal-judge-strikes-down-pennsylvania-same-sex-marriage-ba

Hamer D.(2012 February 14) An open letter on Homosexuality to My Fellow Scientist in Uganda kristof blog.nytimes.com Retrieved from

http://kristof.blogs.nytimes.com/2014/02/20/an-open-letter-on-homosexuality-to-my-fellow-ugandan-scientists/?_php=true&_type=blogs&_r=0

Lincoln, A. (1863, November 19). Gettysburg address, in *Collective Works of Abraham Lincoln: Speeches and Writings,* Balser, R., Ed. Retrieved from

http://www.abrahamlincolnonline.org/lincoln/speeches/gettysburg.htm

Landau J. (2012) The Obama Administration Decision To Defend Constitutional Equality Rather Than The Defense of Marriage Act 81 Fordham L. Rev. 619, Fordham Law Review; retrieved from Westlaw (approx. 19 pages)

http://campus.westlaw.com.lib.kaplan.edu/result/previewcontroller.aspx?TF=756&TC=4&mt=CampusLaw&db=1142&ordoc=2028227528&caseserial=2028227528&rp=%2ffind%2fdefault.wl&findtype=1&spa=004042837-2000&serialnum=0377627421&vr=2.0&fn=_top&sv=Split&pbc=BC6E23F9&casecite=133+S.Ct.+2884&rs=WLW14.04&RP=/find/default.wl&bLinkViewer=true

Johnson C. (1994-2013) MayflowerHistory.com. Retrieved from

http://mayflowerhistory.com/mayflower-compact/

Cal. Const. amend.chap.85.§ § 221.5 (a)(b)(c)(d)(e)(f)

Pa. Const. tit. 23 part II § 1102

Pa. Const. tit. 23 part II § 1704

Or. Const. art. 15, § 5(a)

Oregon v. The United State Supreme Court Case No. 6:13-cv-01834-MC (March 2014)

Tex. Const. art.I § 32(a)

U.S. Declaration of Independence, Paragraph 2 (1776)

1 U.S.C. A. § 7

U. S. Const. Art.I §8 cl.1-20

U.S.Const. art II § 4

U.S.Const. art. III

U.S.Const. amend. I

U.S. Const. amend.X

Utah. Const. art.I. § 29(1)(2)

United States v. Windsor No. 10 CIV. 8435 (June 6, 2012)

(2006) Wis. Const. amend. art. XIII, § 13

Wis.Stat. 108.04(7) (s) 1(b)

www.ingramcontent.com/pod-product-compliance
Lightning Source LLC
Chambersburg PA
CBHW051820210526
45473CB00005B/1681